LOOKING BACK AT
CLASS 40 LOCOMOTIVES

LOOKING BACK AT
CLASS 40 LOCOMOTIVES

Around four and a half years into its service career D205 has been shopped at Doncaster Works in the winter of 1962/3. (Strathwood Library Collection)

Kevin Derrick

AMBERLEY

This edition first published 2016

Amberley Publishing
The Hill, Stroud
Gloucestershire, GL5 4EP

www.amberley-books.com

Copyright © Kevin Derrick, 2016

The right of Kevin Derrick to be identified as
the Author of this work has been asserted in
accordance with the Copyrights, Designs and
Patents Act 1988.

ISBN 978 1 4456 6656 3 (print)
ISBN 978 1 4456 6657 0 (ebook)

British Library Cataloguing in Publication Data.
A catalogue record for this book is available from
the British Library.

Typesetting by Amberley Publishing.
Printed in the UK.

Contents

Introduction

I always had a soft spot for Class 40s or, as they were known, English Electric Type 4s when I first started spotting. This was partly because of their unusual exhaust sound and because they seemed almost exotic to spotters in London as they had migrated north from the Capital's sheds, with only the visits of the regulars to King's Cross to look forward to.

However, day trips to Crewe towarrds the end of the sixties would see a huge number of these big 1Co-Co1s being entered into the notebook. They would be found all over the place it seemed – Crewe South, Crewe Diesel Depot, Crewe North Stabling Point, Crewe station – with them being added to almost all trains for North Wales. Standing close to the concrete footbridge at the north end of Crewe station would ensure that nothing slipped past un-recorded on the goods avoiding lines.

Above: Seen near Bethnal Green in March 1988 when recalling the first run of D200 thirty years before; a suitable headboard has been created to celebrate the locomotive's first express run to Norwich (see opposite). (Strathwood Library Collection)

This page: No. 40194 potters along the Settle & Carlisle at Brinks Hall on 13 April 1982. (Sid Steadman)

Then it would be time to catch your breath and take in a huge number of both Class 47s and Class 40s within Crewe Works for overhaul. A dozen years later and it would be very different if you wanted to just spot dead Class 40s; then you could take your pick from Crewe, Doncaster or Swindon Works as they started accumulating for cutting up.

Most classes of locomotive have their own devotees; it must be said that Class 40s still command an impressive following even after two decades, with only seven of the original 200 Class 40s surviving. Considering the larger numbers of other classes making it to preservation, one does wonder how viable their groups will be in the coming years – perhaps the same might have been said if twice as many Whistlers had survived long enough to be preserved?

From a personal point of view I was glad to have enjoyed the class as part of my spotting days.

Kevin Derrick
Boat of Garten 2010

Draughty
with Discs

Fresh from acceptance trials at Doncaster in March 1958, D200 was prepared to work the first run with a 2,000 hp diesel to Norwich from Liverpool Street, where the press have assembled. (Strathwood Library Collection)

As the earlier class members went through the works, they gained the then new half yellow front warning panels, as demonstrated by D248 on April Fools' Day in 1962. (Strathwood Library Collection)

A fine rake of tanks rumble along behind No. 40093 at Skelton Junction on 27 August 1982. (Strathwood Library Collection)

The steam heat is going well on board No. 40084 at York on 17 April 1982 just before 08.30, the booked departure time for today's Fenman special. (Sid Steadman)

Standing outside in the sun at Derby Works in May 1977 and ready to go out on test was No. 40083. (Tony Shaw)

Having just gone into service earlier in the month, D259, complete with original ladder fixing, runs through Gainsborough Lea road in February 1960. (John Rowe)

Looking back to ensure No. 40052 pulls up correctly for the waiting passengers at Appleby on 18 April 1981 with an S&C stopper. (Sid Steadman)

There are just seven coaches on the drawbar behind No. 40083, seen this time on the viaduct at Welwyn North with the 17.12 King's Cross to Grantham on Wednesday 5 September 1979. (Colin Whitbread)

Tyseley's ex-Great Western Railway water tower on 25 February 1968 provides the backdrop to D291 and D300. (Jerry Beddows)

It is fairly easy to understand that, with the as-built plain green fronts against the light as here on D266 passing Eastfield in 1960, locomotives might not be so easy to see from track level against a hilly or tree background. (Strathwood Library Collection)

The imposing yellow nose of No. 40024 *Lucania*, which is waiting at Carmarthen for a return to Derby with an excursion on 28 April 1984, would be a lot less easy to miss. However, as all drivers knew only too well, the draughts at speed on the road through those front gangway doors could be horrible, and rendered the class unpopular with many drivers. (Stuart Broughton)

The low winter sunlight and characteristic exhaust highlight the profile of No. 40097 in Warrington Arpley Yard on 26 March 1982. (Strathwood Library Collection)

A strange shade of green has been used to touch up No. 254, which is arriving at Doncaster on 19 September 1969. (Strathwood Library Collection)

One of two Class 40s to run without any InterCity arrows was No. 40050, strolling along on 15 October 1982 near Newbiggin on the S&C. The other unbranded locmotive was No. 40157, seen later. (Late Pete Walton/ Sid Steadman)

This was a regular outing most days at this time for D200; eager enthusiasts are on board at Leeds with the 16.00 service train to Carlisle for an enjoyable bit of haulage on 16 August 1983. (Len Ball)

No Rail Blue livery for No. 40106, which became a major celebrity as the last major mainline diesel locomotive still in British Railways green, so much so that management decided to cash in by repainting it green and using it for exhibition and railtour work. It certainly was a refreshing change in that short-lived sea of blue locomotives at the time when seen at Upperby on 5 July 1980. (Sid Steadman)

Keeping a careful eye on his train at Appleby was the driver of No. 40056 in May 1984. (Pete Walton/ Sid Steadman)

Class 40s were regulars for over a decade on most freights over the Settle & Carlisle; towards the end of this glorious reign we find No. 40093 on 12 May 1981 passing over the road crossing that gives access to the village of Culgaith. (Sid Steadman)

During its spell in blue livery No. 200 accelerates a rake of Presflos through Arpley Junction at Warrington on 23 March 1972. (Jeffrey Lane)

Compared with No. 200 on the previous page, D207, which was one of the early blue repaints, has a smaller size set of InterCity arrows when captured at Wigan on 6 April 1968. (Grahame Wareham)

The distinctive engine note of an approaching Class 40 under load heralded the appearance in the viewfinder of D291 near Tebay on 28 June 1965. (Strathwood Library Collection)

More of that differing shade of green paint, most likely from a two-tone green Brush Type 4, has been used to touch in D270, which is stabled at March on 24 January 1965. The coaling tower, that one time landmark across the flat Fenland, still stands proud in the background, but not for much longer. (Eric Sawford/Stewart Blencowe Collection)

Well turned-out but very much unloved by steam men at the time, D267 has command of the Royal Scot near Bare Lane in 1961, having deposed Stanier's Duchesses from the train. It was suggested that some of the old hands at Camden during 1960 and 1961 would seek to deliberately fail their English Electric Type 4 in favour of a steam replacement for one more fling. (Strathwood Library Collection)

Making steady progress up towards Shap near Shap Wells on 18 July 1964 was D268, the driver having ensured that the engine room doors and rear cab window were thrown open to prevent the build up of fumes. (Richard Icke)

Crossing back over at Bare Lane was D310 during 1963. This locomotive was delivered new in early December 1960. (Strathwood Library Collection)

This fine photograph of No. 201 was taken on 17 October 1971 on the traverser at Crewe Works. The glade of overhaul required would determine whether the locomotive would gain a coat of Rail Blue. Glimpsed in the background is at least one Class 47 returning to traffic, still in two-tone green livery. (Frank Hornby)

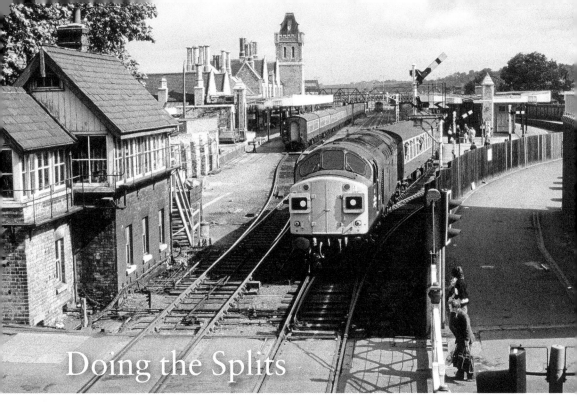

Doing the Splits

A compromise design for both Class 40s and the Peaks saw split headcode boxes applied to them both when new in small batches. One such machine, No. 40129, gets away from Lincoln on its way to Manchester on 3 September 1983. (Stuart Broughton)

Released from its stock No. 40130 will set off to clear the platforms at Liverpool Lime Street on 28 June 1980. (Ian James)

Tucked away in a corner of the main erecting shop within Crewe Works on 10 February 1979 was No. 40142, looking ready to go back into traffic. (Aldo Delicata)

Sweeping through Carnforth station in 1965 was D332. *Brief Encounter* was filmed here in the 1940s with Celia Johnson and Trevor Howard. (Len Smith)

Whistling steadily around the curves through Chester with a Down Freightliner on 23 June 1980 was No. 40135. Having been built by English Electric at Vulcan Foundry, Newton-le-Willows, during early 1961, she entered service on 11 March 1961, allocated to 5A Crewe North. In April 1966 the allocation was recorded as Western Lines, and then from June 1968 to D05 Stoke Division; May 1969 to D09 Manchester Division; Jan. 1972 to D08 Liverpool Division; May 1973 to Springs Branch; August 1973 to Carlisle Kingmoor; and May 1975 to Longsight, where she remained until withdrawal on 22 January 19 1985.

From this point, the locomotive led something of a charmed life. Thanks to behind the scenes intervention, the loco had a very close call with the cutter's torch at Doncaster Works. Having survived scrapping, she was one of four Class 40 station miraculously returned to departmental traffic in May 1985, for use in the re-modelling of Crewe station approaches. Based at Crewe Diesel TMD and renumbered to No. 97406, she and the other three 97s worked around Crewe and on various other freight duties in the London Midland Region.

Final withdrawal from British Rail service came on 16 December 1986. Thankfully, further intervention prevented the loco from reaching Swindon Works for scrapping. After painstaking negotiations and discussions, No. 40135 was put onto the BR tender list, along with No. 40012. The Class 40 Preservation Society successfully tendered for the loco in May 1988, and she began a life in preservation. (John Arthur Bennett/Strathwood Library Collection)

Once locomotives were being repainted from green such as D342 here at Wigan Springs Branch on 21 March 1968, that bright red bufferbeam disappeared. The new scheme saw the use of black instead. (Strathwood Library Collection)

The all yellow front end paintwork on D340 at Carlisle in September 1972 looks pretty fresh. (Arthur Wilson)

Class 40s were to be used for a good number of years as the main source of traction for a high number of the day returns in the excursion market to and from Blackpool, which is where we find No. 40143 on 21 April 1984. (Phil Bidwell)

Centres of Attention

With that distictive engine note whistling away and carrying along the banks of the River Eden, close by to Carlisle Kingmoor depot, on 28 June 1981, No. 40154 is today engaged on permanent way duties as the engineers have possession of the line. (Sid Steadman)

This might just be the first time down the East Coast Main Line for D394, which is near Gamston in June 1962. Records show that this Class 40 entered traffic from 52A Gateshead on the 13th of the month. (Colour-Rail)

For over twenty years the sound of Class 40s reverberating around the environs of Manchester Victoria was commonplace. On 9 September 1981 No. 40169 was most likely just one of several of the class to grace the station during the day. (Mark McDermott/Strathwood Libarary Collection)

The fine array of semaphore signals around Ely would draw many cameramen to this Fenland location, and a bonus would be the sights and sounds of No. 40198 wrestling an engineer's special through the station on 24 March 1982. (Phil Bidwell)

Running light around the yards at Warrington on 7 April 1983, No. 40145 seemed nothing special aside from being one of the surviving Class 40s still at work. However the following month saw it derailed in Stourton Yard in Leeds and, as a result, withdrawn from service. Unlike so many of its sisters it was not be sent to Swindon, Crewe or Doncaster for cutting up. Instead the Class 40 Preservation Society, which had been formed to secure a locomotive of their own, went for this example and in February 1984 it moved to a new home on the East Lancashire Railway at Bury. (Stuart Broughton)

The approach to patching up Class 40s at Crewe works during the late 1960s and early 1970s – a quick touch up and back into service in green paint if possible – meant that several specimens were to be renumbered into TOPS before any repaints into Rail Blue could take place. One such locomotive was No. 40171 which was among those stabled at Guide Bridge on 26 June 1976. (Derek Everson)

A lengthy parcels train draws into York during the 1960s with a reasonably smart D355 at its head. (Strathwood Library Collection)

Another lengthy train is in behind the drawbar of D392 at Farrington Junction on 16 May 1962. At this time the locomotive was in its first month of service and shedded at 52A Gateshead, so perhaps it was a stranger on the WCML? (Chris Forrest)

It's steady progress for No. 40169 on the approach to Totley Tunnel East on 18 May 1975. When new in December 1961 it was first allocated to Crewe 5A for acceptance; once complete she would take up duties from 1B Camden for the next four years. (Jeffrey Lane)

Just a few of the class gained crudely affixed running numbers to their noses towards the end of their service days, which were sometimes a convenience to cameramen in recognising the actual engine number when their shots came back from developing. No such need here as our photographer had taken notes on No. 40170's visit to Sheffield Midland in June 1982. (David T. Williams)

One of those examples of Crewe Works patch-ups towards the end of the sixties and early seventies, with D383 under test before a return to traffic. (Strathwood Library Collection)

The exhausts betray No. 40183, which is under full power passing the Fox's mints factory at Ashton during May 1982. Just a few weeks later she would be set aside and withdrawn on 14 June 1982. Sent to Crewe shortly after, the Class 40 would linger around until early April 1984 before all trace of it had gone. (Late Pete Walton/Sid Steadman)

A crew change at Doncaster allowed a chance to take this view of No. 40150 on 21 May 1981. (Sid Steadman)

The early service years for a number of the class would be on the southern reaches of the West Coast Main Line until electrification progressively forced the class further north as the wires went up. Pictured is Willesden shed before the masts went up, with D382 on shed. Along with a number of classmates they saw off many of Sir William Stanier's finest steam locomotives, perhaps before their time. (Strathwood Library Collection)

Going well in March 1982 and requiring a panning action to capture a shot was No. 40181 near Helm. (Sid Steadman)

No need for any panning at Preston le Skerne on 7 May 1965 as D350 is not going anywhere soon – well, not until the engineers turn up with some cranes to get her back out of the cess. The mishap occured two days previously when the Gateshead locomotive passed a signal at danger, before running through the catch points and down the embankment, landing on its side in soft ground. Its train then jackknifed everywhere, fouling the mainline. The next train to arrive on the scene before the signals could be thrown to danger on other lines was D352, in charge of a Manchester–Newcastle newspaper service, which collided with a number of the wagons. In a crazy coincidence a nearby field saw a USAF jet crash land a few days later! (Noel Marrison)

North Wales Routes

A Llandudno–Euston via Birmingham New Street service has No. 40012 *Aureol* up front and making good progress at Greenfield on 26 July 1980. (John Arthur Bennet/Strathwood Library Collection)

On 30 August 1984 the train sheds at Chester play host to No. 40044 with a parcels working. This must be considered a very fortunate Class 40, as a collision rendered it out of traffic at Crewe Works from September 1978 until March 1980, when repairs were completed for a return to traffic. Taken out of service on 22 January 1985, perhaps the expenditure for repairs was justified? (Strathwood Library Collection)

Class 40s enjoyed a number of years working the Freightliner trains along the North Wales coastal route to and from Holyhead. One such working on the morning of 3 July 1982 has No. 40170 taking the Chester slow lines. (John Arthur Bennet/Strathwood Library Collection)

The 09.00 Llandudno–York service has No. 40108 in charge on 14 June 1980; two months later the locomotive would be withdrawn. (Colin Whitbread)

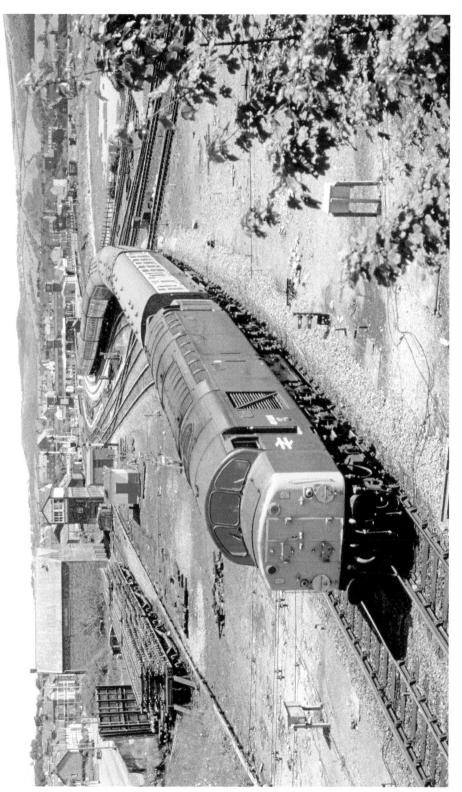

Going the other way on 27 June 1981 was No. 40006 with the 08.55 York and Sheffield Midland–Llandudno service at Llandudno Junction. (Colin Whitbread)

Having lost the train reporting discs and gained a painted name once more, along with the running number on the nose, No. 40012 *Aureol* is at Chester on 14 August 1982 with the 08.41 to Manchester Victoria. (John Arthur Bennet/Strathwood Library Collection)

A light engine movement for No. 40013 *Andania* on 24 May 1981 through Chester. (John Arthur Bennet/Strathwood Library Collection)

Again stripped of its discs is No. 40121 on 28 August 1982, when we find it at Llandudno ready to head the 13.53 departure to York. (Len Ball)

On its way back from Llandudno to Crewe with a returning excursion was No. 40116 near Chester on 28 June 1980 in its last year in traffic. (John Arthur Bennet/Strathwood Library Collection)

Underwired 40s

A rake of parcels vans follows No. 40013 *Andania* into Guide Bridge on 2 September 1982. (Strathwood Library Collection)

In July 1981 several spotters take Gateshead's No. 40068 for granted at Birmingham New Street; it has two years' further service and a transfer to Healey Mills still to come. (David T. Williams)

Preston is the location of this shot of a Northwich–Corkickle working for No. 40141 on 7 October 1976. (Len Ball)

Class 40s were a regular fixture at London's King's Cross for many years; however now that wires were up and the Deltics were gone the writing was on the wall for No. 40069, which had ventured to the Capital on 27 October 1982. (Late Derek Whitnell/Strathwood Library Collection)

A very tatty No. 40136, based at Longsight and about to be transferred to Carlisle Kingmoor, keeps the M6 motorway to the north in its sights as it runs light engine near Bescot in July 1976. (David T. Williams)

By October 1984 any arrivals of Class 40s into New Street would be worthy of a photograph; here No. 40086 backs on to its train three months before being struck off from service. (David T. Williams)

The driver of No. 40198 looks back along his train at Preston to check all is as it should be in around 1980. (Strathwood Library Collection)

There is more Class 40 activity at King's Cross with No. 40058 arrived at the stops on Saturday 6 September 1980. (Colin Whitbread)

On 24 June 1981 it was an empty stock working for No. 40025 *Lusitania* under the differing forms of catenary at Stockport. (Colin Whitbread)

One could even see the odd Western Class 52 at Birmingham New Street when this shot of No. 40081 was recorded in June 1976. While the hydraulics were almost over, the Class 40s would struggle on for another decade. (David T. Williams)

Taken from the platform ends at Lime Street our cameraman would have been able to watch No. 40130 approach for some time through the cuttings bringing the tracks into Liverpool city centre on 28 June 1980. (Ian James)

This locomotive became infamous after that August night in 1963 when it was rostered to haul the 18.50. Up special Travelling Post Office from Glasgow Central to Euston on the 7th. The newspapers around the world would be proclaiming headlines all about 'The Great Train Robbery' for decades whenever the opportunity arose. This view was taken at Willesden in Augsut 1967 and shows the locomotive as one the earlier examples to be painted with a full yellow warning panel from the split headcode batch. It was its notable history that ensured British Rail management's decree that it would be quickly cut up on arrival at Swindon on 29 March 1984 with barely a trace left a fortnight later, just in case anyone had the notion of saving it. (Strathwood Library Collection)

Management had no desire to save the Woodhead route either, where we see No. 40020 *Franconia* at Guide Bridge along with Nos 76011 and 76021 on a special on 3 May 1980. (John Arthur Bennet/Strathwood Library Collection)

Further along the No. 1500 volt DC route across the Pennines we find No. 40012 *Aureol* at Nunnery sidings in Sheffield with ECS from Doncaster in the late morning of 13 September 1977. (Jeffrey Lane)

As one of the later survivors No. 40012 *Aureol* managed to fight its way into many enthusiasts' photographic collections and the selection for this book as we find it arriving at Warrington Bank Quay on 14 August 1982. Ultimately its luck would run out and, with derailment damage, it was withdrawn on 8 February three years later, being sent to Crewe, as many of her sisters had been, for disposal. However all was not lost, as she was mercifully reinstated to departmental traffic as No. 97407 during May 1985 for use on permanent way trains involved in remodelling Crewe's track layout.

With these duties over she was withdrawn once again on 4 April 1986 and fortunately purchased by the Class 40 Appeal in June 1988. *Aureol* was first restarted on 18 October 1992, and her first passenger train working in preservation was made on 17 July 1993.

Since preservation No. 40012 has graced a number of rail centres and private railways for open days and galas. The loco had serious bogie frame fractures at the end of her British Rail days, like many of her compatriots. So it was that the Class 40 Appeal faced real problems in March 1995 when No. 40012 failed a main line inspection for the return journey after visiting the Mid Hants Railway, despite passing the inspection for the outward journey. The situation effectively resulted in a movement 'ban' from the main line after her eventual return, restricting the loco from visiting other railways.

Fortunately things improved and No. 40012 joined fellow preserved 40s Nos 40135 and 40145 at Basford Hall Open Day in August 1994. This was the first ever gathering of three preserved Class 40s, and the first time in several years that three operational Class 40s had been in one location. (Phil Bidwell)

Another Class 40 is at Nunnery siding, with No. 40084 leaving for Longsight with ECS on 24 March 1982, ending its service as a Healey Mills locomotive on 29 May the following spring. (Jeffrey Lane)

Well turned out for traffic at Birmingham New Street in June 1983 was No. 40177, keeping company with No. 86315, one of the Doncaster Works-built Class 86s as opposed to one of the English Electric Vulcan Foundry-built machines. (David T. Williams)

Venuturing back under the wires from Crewe Diesel Depot during October 1970 was No. 331, which had the original style of numbering painted out and replaced with new numerals. (Strathwood Library Collection)

Namers

One of earliest of the named 40s in blue was D233 *Empress of England* which is going well at Long Preston with a fitted freight on 28 June 1968. This blue repaint was a legacy of use with No. 216 *Campania* to double head the Prince of Wales's Royal Train for his investiture at Caernarvon in 1969. This Class 40 was named within Derby Works on 9 September 1961 after the Canadian Pacific Line vessel of the same name, which had been launched on the Tyne in May 1956. (Douglas Twibell/Transport Treasury)

Based within D08, the Liverpool Division, for much of the late 1960s, we find D224 *Lucania* working into south-west Scotland at Kilmarnock. New into traffic on 15 August 1959, it would run nameless until August 1962, when those distinctive nameplates were fitted at Crewe Works. (Arthur Wilson)

Still proudly carrying her nameplates at Garston on 30 April 1974 was No. 40022 *Laconia*, which had just been outshopped from Crewe earlier in the month and renumbered into TOPS on release. (Phil Bidwell)

Accelerating away from the staion at Manchester Victoria on 21 August 1979 was No. 40033 *Empress* of *England* with an interim painting of the name, which was later painted onto a red background. (Len Ball)

Named as *Campania* in May 1962 after almost three years' service was D216, captured at Crewe on 25 February 1967. (Strathwood Library Collection)

From a vantage point near Carlisle we see D232 *Empress of Canada* in firm control of the 10.40 Glasgow Central–Birmingham New Street service on 4 October 1967. The arrivals of Class 50s from Vulcan Foundry in the next twelve months would see Class 40s working fewer and fewer of these services north of Crewe as the new arrivals took over. (Douglas Twibell/Transport Treasury)

Heavy snow along the Settle & Carlisle route on 15 February 1979 will impede the progress of No. 40017 *Carinthia*, which has been brought to a stand at Appleby. (Sid Steadman)

Whistling away at the buffer stops at Manchester Piccadilly we catch up with No. 40034 *Accra* on 28 June 1980; like so many after the early seventies, it is devoid of nameplates. (Ian James)

Cleaned up with a partial repaint in this works visit to Crewe was D213 *Andania* on 26 February 1967. (Strathwood Library Collection)

Rolling a Cleethorpes–Manchester service into Doncaster on 27 August 1981 was No. 40028 *Samaria*. (Strathwood Library Collection)

A Class 25 is on banking duty on 24 April 1984 to assist No. 40035 *Apapa* up Miles Platting bank out of Manchester Victoria. (Stuart Broughton)

Looking very workaday on a light engine movement at Carlisle in 1967 was D221 *Ivernia*. (Douglas Twibell/ Transport Treasury)

Starting out from Crewe on the morning of 3 May 1980 was No. 40020 *Franconia*, which would take the SLOA-organised tour The Mancunian here from Manchester Piccadilly to meet the Midland Compound, *Green Arrow* and *Sir Nigel Gresley* for a jaunt behind steam from Leeds. (John Arthur Bennet/Strathwood Library Collection)

It was a desire to improve timings north of the border further during the 1960s as Stanier's steam fleet gave way to Class 40s such as D210 *Empress of Britain*, which is seen crossing the infant River Clyde at Crawford around 1965. Three years later and Class 50s would be used first singly, then in pairs as the seventies began, before giving way to the electrics. (Strathwood Library Collection)

A real favourite for many Class 40 fans was No. 40025 *Lusitania*, seen here getting away from Doncaster during 1981. (Arthur Wilson)

All is not well on board No. 40029 *Saxonia* as she struggles with the 13.30 Sheffield Nunnery–Manchester Longsight ECS working on 5 April 1983. (Jeffrey Lane)

40 Below

A bitingly cold day on the Settle & Carlisle near Settle Junction greets No. 40090 in December 1981. (Late Pete Walton/Sid Steadman)

Making its way around Crewe North stabling point in the winter of 1967 was D324. (Strathwood Library Collection)

A short freight booked to Warcop in the snow of 26 February 1986 and in the hands of D200 was enough temptation to venture out into the snow on a sunny day on the S&C to record the scene. (Late Pete Walton/ Sid Steadman)

Several withdrawn Class 40s, including No. 40099, were stored out in the cold at Kingmoor during the winter of 1984/5, awaiting their call to meet the scrappers. (Sid Steadman)

Heavyweight Scrap

Visits to Crewe Works from the early 1960s onwards would always bring a wide selection of Class 40s to record while they were undergoing repairs. However, as the 1970s rolled into the 1980s, the works were always littered with dead Whistlers such as No. 40091 on 4 July 1987. (Strathwood Library Collection)

Taken out of service on 3 October 1982 this unfortunate locomotive was stored firstly at Stratford before a place was made at Doncaster for it. By 14 July 1985 the scrap men had taken a few hearty nibbles out of No. 40094. (Colin Whitbread)

Spotters seize a chance to explore the insides of No. 40169 at Doncaster Works on 18 July 1984. (Strathwood Library Collection)

The 'Melts Shop' within Crewe Works would consume a varied diet of scrap locomotives over the years; next on the menu on 2 June 1984 would be No. 40188. (Steve Barnes)

Also for the chop at Crewe were No. 40195 in July 1987 and No. 40088 in June 1984. (Both: David T. Williams)

Crash-damaged No. 40142 makes a plea
for mercy for its classmates at Crewe
in June 1981. (Strathwood Library
Collection)

Swindon's cutting staff make swift work of what's left of No. 40110 on 16 September 1983 after the locomotive's entrails had been removed within the main erecting shop, now more a place of destruction. (Steve Barnes)

Judging by the cutting lines already begun on No. 40037 at the same spot on 2 November 1983 the same method of dismantling will be followed closely from No. 40110 above. (Steve Barnes)

Visitors to the works wander through the lines of locomotives at Swindon for scrap, which include Nos 40026 and 46030 on 6 June 1981. (Strathwood Library Collection)

Awaiting the call at Doncaster Works in August 1984 was No. 40170. (Alister Betts)

Our friend from the ditch at Preston le Skerne on page 34, D350, now as No. 40150, is not going to escape this time. Stripped at Crewe, the 'Melts Shop' awaits in February 1986. (Strathwood Library Collection)

On the Double

Two unknown pairings out on the sands at Arnside on 5 May 1980. (Colin Whitbread)

The trackside rosebay willowherb lends a splash of colour to Nos 40186 and 40195 in June 1980 at Kirby Stephen. (Late Pete Walton/Sid Steadman)

It's one for the accountants to sharpen their pencils when working out the viability of this working of Nos 40001 and 40098 and a single brake on the S&C in May 1976. (Richard Griffiths)

Up front is D340, which has failed on a Birmingham–Edinburgh service. The steam banker was having a hard time keeping things going from Tebay towards Shap, and D316 on the following Euston–Perth service moved up and pushed the ensemble to the summit from Scout Green on 25 July 1964. (Chris Forrest)

The loading on 7 December 1980 on the Red Bank vans was light for No. 40128 with No. 40133 at Culgaith. (Sid Steadman)

You can wait ages for one doubleheader only for two to turn up at the same time, as here at Chester on Saturday 27 June 1981 with No. 40129 piloting No. 47437 on ECS while Nos 25199 and 25048 work a tanker duty. (Colin Whitbread)

Matched today with No. 56029, this strange pairing for No. 40157, one of the two Class 40s running without InterCity arrows, draws the 15.01 Fiddlers Ferry–Healey Mills service away from Warrington on 18 June 1982. (Len Ball)

Catching the low evening sun at Stockber on the Settle & Carlisle were Nos 40146 and 40075 on 29 May 1980. (Sid Steadman)

An interesting combination again this time with No. 40196 assisting No. 37048 at Ormside on the Up line in April 1983. (Late Pete Walton/Sid Steadman)

Forty
Nights

Pressed into use for an evening King's Cross–Edinburgh service on 19 May 1981, No. 40024 *Lucania* makes a stop heading north at Doncaster. (Sid Steadman)

Another East Coast Main Line duty for a Class 40, as No. 40057 waits to get away from Newcastle with the 21.00 for King's Cross on 26 November 1981. (Colin Whitbread)

Postal traffic is being loaded aboard No. 40122's train at Carlisle Citadel station in the early evening of 29 March 1985. (Late Pete Walton/Sid Steadman)

Dealing with the ECS off a Middlesborough to King's Cross football special was No. 31226, having brought fans to a fixture with Arsenal on Saturday 20 September 1980. Meanwhile, No. 40069 stands alongside with a newspaper train at the London terminus. (Colin Whitbread)

Another view of No. 40057 on 26 November 1981 at Newcastle Central waiting to move onto its train to King's Cross. (Colin Whitbread)

The yard lights at Toton illuminate No. 40177 right at the end of its working life on 2 May 1984, with just two more months left in service. (Stuart Broughton)

A Few Variations

The distinctive No. 40069, with its lower body side cut away for easier access, waits at Chester on 14 June 1980. (Colin Whitbread)

Seen broadside at Haymarket, No. 40157 has no InterCity arrows on either side on 1 March 1980. (Len Ball)

Among the thirty-three class members to have their boiler water tanks removed in later years was No. 40196, standing at Toton on 2 February 1983. (Stuart Broughton)

Some of the early examples into service were fitted with a ladder to assist footplate staff to reach up and clean the forward windows. Still eighteen months away from being named *Lancastria*, D223 stands with ladders in place at Willesden on 20 September 1959. It was decided, after a few unfortunate accidents with staff coming into contact with the overhead, that these ladders should be removed completely. (Frank Hornby)

At least fourteen of the class would give up their discs later in their careers, usually due to corrosion in the hinges, encouraging fitting staff to remove them completely. This has happened to No. 40003, which is at Sutton Bridge Junction, Shrewsbury, on 18 April 1981. (Ian James)

Running through Sheffield Midland on its journey from Doncaster with the 11.15 service to Nunnery Sidings on 16 April 1983 was No. 40044. (Len Ball)

Several locomotives had their centre doors sealed shut at one or both ends. The No. 2 end of No. 40139 had this treatment when pictured here at Scarborough on 25 July 1981 with a train for Manchester Victoria, after most likely suffering light collision damage. (Colin Whitbread)

Unlike No. 40139 seen previously, No. 40144 has had the lamp and headboard brackets removed as well when it was recorded at Llandudno on 30 June 1979. (Colin Whitbread)

Another variation to keep class memebers running saw No. 40127 gain doors from a withdrawn disc-fitted locomotive at the No. 2 end only. On 20 May 1980 it was making its way through Bold with empty tanks for Stanlow. (John Arthur Bennet/Strathwood Library Collection)

The No. 2 end of No. 40158 gained a repair to its headcode box in the style of the Deltics, viewed here arriving at Birmingham New Street in June 1983. (David T. Williams)

Another style of headcode blanking was fitted to No. 40062, on test at Edinburgh Waverley. Notably, this machine started life as a disc headcode locomotive and was one of the seven Scottish Region central headcode conversions carried out in the 1960s. (Albert C. Greig)

Another of these Scottish Region conversions was No. 40063 near Mallerstang on 22 July 1982. The giveaway is the drop down waistline where the original gangway doors were *in situ* and welded up. Three of these Haymarket-based 40s had rounded headcode panels rather than this type with squared corners. (Late Pete Walton/Sid Steadman)

The simple lettering of No. 40022's nameplate. (Phil Bidwell)

Much more is incorporated on No. 40010. (Strathwood Library Collection)

Bolts remain, but the once-fine nameplate is now a simple painted version on No. 40012 by 1982. (John Arthur Bennet/Strathwood Library Collection)

The reinstated No. 40060 carried this decoration for a while, running as No. 97405. (Strathwood Library Collection)

This painted nameplate theme extended to unofficial names such as on No. 40104, which became *Warrior*. It is stabled here at Carlisle on 29 September 1984. (Arthur Wilson)

Left: The once-official name of No. 40035 was crudely reinstated when seen at Inverness during 1979. (Phil Bidwell)

Right: A simple stencil version was applied to No. 40137, seen on 6 June 1981. (Aldo Delicata)

By the time No. 40128 had reached Doncaster for cutting up in May 1983, she was carrying all sorts of extra painted details. (Strathwood Library Collection)

40s on Tour

It's a day out around the sunny south for No. 40179 on 1 February 1978 for the DAA and DEG-organised Whistler Railtour taking in much of the Southern Region's Central Section coastal destinations, including Havant, where we catch up with the train. (Bernard Mills)

On 17 April 1982 a circuitous route from Leeds to Liverpool Street and back brought No. 40084 to March as part of the Class 40 Preservation Society's Fenman railtour. (Late Pete Walton/Sid Steadman)

A Peak and a Class 50 keep No. 40044 company in April 1984, although it is the Class 40 that has drawn the crowd. (David T. Williams)

An impressive tour headboard is carried by No. 40035 *Apapa* at Craven Arms on 3 March 1984. The tour also had haulage from Nos 37266, 37300, 50001 and 45064 during the day, with No. 37266 and the Peak supporting the tour to provide some heating at times to the hopefully grateful passengers. (Phil Bidwell)

Saturday 20 September 1980 saw No. 40028 *Samaria* take a turn on the railtour circuit with a trip from King's Cross to Lincolnshire and the North East, utilising Nos 08373, 20015, 20076, 37101 and 37143 through the day. Standing alongside on arrival back in the Capital was No. 55005 *The Prince of Wales's Own Regiment* of Yorkshire on the 19.55 from York. (Colin Whitbread)

Steam heat aplenty for Nos 40057 and 40135, which have combined to form 'The Devonian' at Bristol Temple Meads on 28 May 1984. (Steve Feltham)

Doubleheaded Class 40s again on 13 May 1985 with Nos 40122 and 40091 paused at Ribblehead while working with eighteen other locomotives as part of the three-day tour that was Skirl o' the Pipes 4. (Phil Bidwell)

The Dore Mat on 18 February 1984 enjoys haulage from No. 40024 *Lucania* at Sheffield Midland, the tour used No. 40033 *Empress of England* for several legs and even No. 13001, one of Tinsley's hump shunters. (Stuart Broughton)

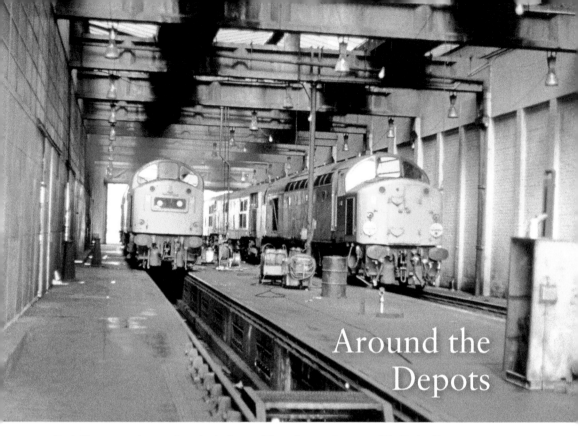

Around the
Depots

Both Nos 40152 and 40038 share the facilities at Thornaby on 18 June 1979. (Phil Bidwell)

One of the locations around Liverpool where the class were once commonplace as here on 12 August 1979 with No. 40136 taking in the sun at Birkenhead. (Phil Bidwell)

A replacement buffer has been installed on No. 40159 at Eastfield around 1980. (Albert Greig)

Early days for the class provided 30A Statford with a healthy allocation to work expresses from Liverpool Street as steam was being phased out on 7 October 1960. (Late Vincent Heckford/Strathwood Library Collection)

Towards the last days of the class, some of them would be stored and have minor works visits to Stratford, keeping them in touch with the former Great Eastern routes. At Colchester on 19 August 1980 spotters would find No. 40181 laid over. (Phil Bidwell)

Some serious work being carried out inside at Wigan to No. 40132 on 27 September 1980. (Steve Barnes)

Thirty-four class members remained in green livery when their TOPS numbers were applied; among these was No. 40136, which, by 26 June 1976, was more than a little weatherbeaten when found at Newton Heath. (Derek Everson)

There is a better presentation to be enjoyed in the external condition of No. 40177 inside the maintenance shed at Inverness on 20 April 1977. (Nev Sloper)

The vast inside accomodation available at Toton sees No. 40024 *Lucania* here for maintenance work on 4 February 1983. (Stuart Broughton)

This was one of the Scottish Region's headcode conversions with rounded edges; although officially withdrawn on 22 January 1985, it remained active on local freight work around Carlisle with dispensation for some time into 1985. We find it on shed at Kingmoor while still active. (Late Pete Walton/Sid Steadman)

Longsight keeps No. 40168 going for a few more short months on 20 June 1984. (Steve Feltham)

This was more the regular domain of English Electric Class 37s, but among those on shed on 12 October 1980 was No. 40017 *Carinthia*, adding a little variety. (Phil Bidwell)

Another of those locomotives with flush-welded front gangway doors was No. 40111, which waits for another run away from York on 22 May 1981. (Sid Steadman)